KU-626-803

On the FARM

Illustrated by
Sally Hobson

WALKER BOOKS
AND SUBSIDIARIES
LONDON · BOSTON · SYDNEY

Whose
webby
feet
are these?

broom
broom

Whose
red
tractor
is this?

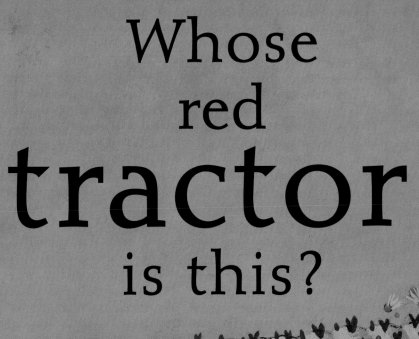

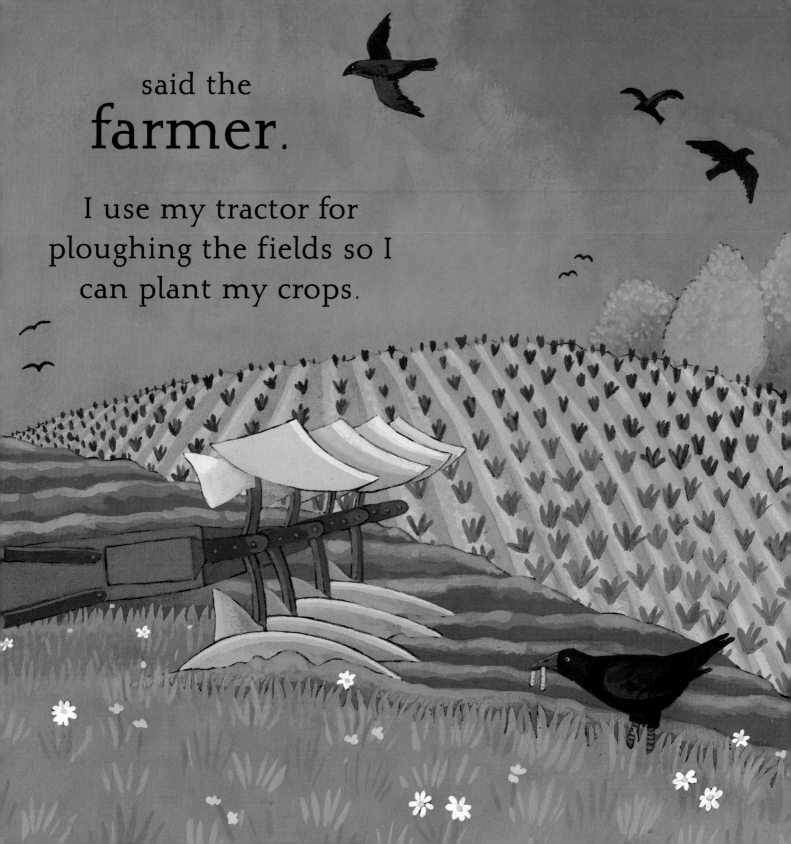

said the
farmer.

I use my tractor for
ploughing the fields so I
can plant my crops.

Whose little babies are these?

...ig.

...are
...milk
...ow.

baa
baa

crack
crack

Whose woolly sheep are these?

moo
moo

Whose
long
tail
is this?

Here we are, on the farm.
Can you find the duck, the farmer,
the pig, the shepherd, the hen
and the cow?

Whose brown eggs are these?

First published 2000 by Walker Books Ltd
87 Vauxhall Walk, London SE11 5HJ

2 4 6 8 10 9 7 5 3 1

Series concept and design by Louise Jackson

Words by Paul Harrison and Louise Jackson

Wildlife consultant: Martin Jenkins

Text © 2000 Walker Books Ltd
Illustrations © 2000 Sally Hobson

This book has been typeset in Calligraphic.

Printed in Thailand

British Library Cataloguing in Publication Data
A catalogue record for this book is available
from the British Library.

ISBN 0-7445-6245-7